A Kid's Guide to
Costa Rica

Two Scarlet Macaws, native to Costa Rica

Jack L. Roberts

Curious Kids Press • Palm Springs, CA
www.curiouskidspress.com

Publisher: *Curious Kids Press, Palm Springs, CA 92264. All rights reserved.*
Editor: *Sterling Moss*
Designed by: *Michael Owens*
Copy Editor: *Janice Ross*

Table of Contents

Welcome to Costa Rica.. 4

Your Passport to Costa Rica..5

Where in the World Is Costa Rica..6

The 7 Central American Countries.................................... 7

A Brief History of Costa Rica 8

6 Cool Facts About Costa Rica...9

Life in Costa Rica: Pura Vida... 10

How to Speak Spanish in Costa Rica...............................11

What's to Eat: The Food in Costa Rica............................12

Christmas Tamales...13

School and Money in Costa Rica.......................................14

Holidays in Costa Rica 15

Tico-style Bullfighting...16

Costa Rican Wildlife...17

The Rainforests of Costa Rica...18

Monkey Around in Costa 20

National Hero: Juan Santamaria....................................... 24

Glossary...25

Other CKP Books...27

For Parents and Teachers..28

Welcome to Costa Rica

"Bienvenido"
(bee-en-veh-nee-doh)

"IMAGINE ZOOMING ACROSS the top of a rainforest on a canopy zip-line. Or getting an up-close look at the smoking crater of a volcano. Or taking pictures of troops of squirrel monkeys swinging from tree branch to tree branch in the jungle. Those are just some of the thrilling activities that kids and their families can enjoy when they visit my beautiful and tropical country – *COSTA RICA.*"

Background photo: Central American Squirrel Monkey

Your Passport to Costa Rica

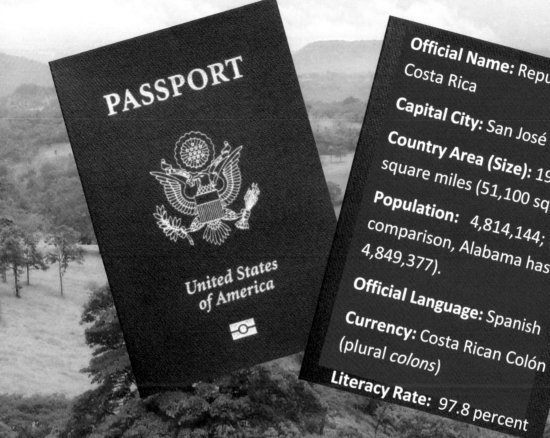

Official Name: Republic of Costa Rica

Capital City: San José

Country Area (Size): 19,730 square miles (51,100 sq. km)

Population: 4,814,144; (By comparison, Alabama has 4,849,377).

Official Language: Spanish

Currency: Costa Rican Colón (plural *colons*)

Literacy Rate: 97.8 percent

The official flag of Costa Rica consists of five horizontal bars of blue, white, red, white, and blue. The National Coat of Arms is on the red band. Each color represents (or stands for) different things. Blue represents religious ideals. White symbolizes happiness, wisdom, and peace. Red stands for the warmth of the Costa Rican people, and blood spilled during their fight for independence.

Background photo: Costa Rica landscape

Where in the World Is Costa Rica?

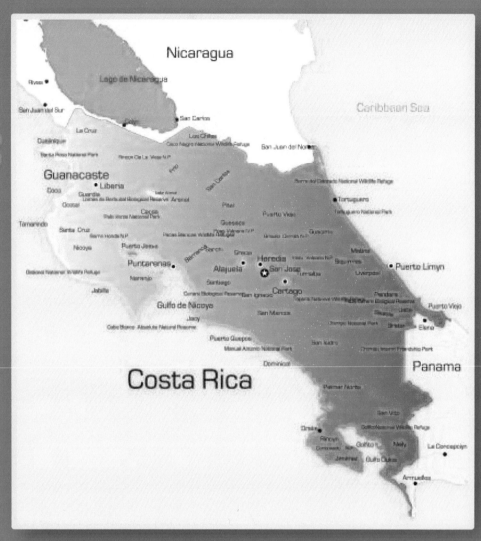

COSTA RICA IS ONE of seven countries in **Central America**. It is located between Nicaragua to the north and Panama to the southeast. It also lies between the Pacific Ocean to the west and the Caribbean Sea to the east.

Costa Rica is not a very big country. In fact, it's slightly smaller than West Virginia. But it gets more tourists each year than any other Central American country.

The 7 Central American Countries

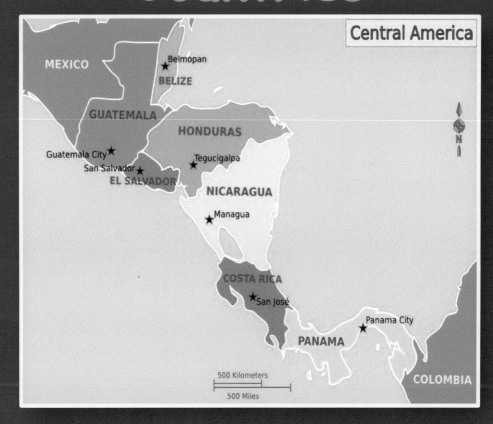

WANT AN EASY WAY to remember the seven countries of Central America? Here's one way. It's called a mnemonic. (Say: nee-MON-ik, the M is silent.) It's a way to help you remember lots of different things, like – well – a list of the seven Central American countries.

Look at the silly sentence below. The first letter of each word in this mnemonic stands for one of the seven Central American countries. Just remember that sentence and you'll always remember the countries. Can you think of other funny mnemonics for the seven countries?

Big Guys Eat Hamburgers Not Canned Peanuts!
(Belize, Guatemala, El Salvador, Honduras, Nicaragua, Costa Rica, Panama)

A Brief History of Costa Rica

1502 Christopher Columbus lands on the coast of Costa Rica.

1524 Explorers from Spain establish the first European colony in Costa Rica.

1821 Costa Rica declares its independence from Spain.

1852 The National Anthem of Costa Rica is composed.

1869 Costa Rica becomes a democracy.

1945 Costa Rica becomes the 44th member of the United Nations.

1948 Costa Rica abolishes (does away with) its army.

1949 Women and people of African descent gain the right to vote.

2010 Costa Rica elects its first woman president.

Did You Know?

Franklin Chang Diaz was the first Costa Rican-born American in space.

Chang Diaz was born in San José, Costa Rica. He became an American citizen in 1977. In 1986, he became the first Costa Rican-born American astronaut in space.

Cool Facts About Costa Rica

Every Costa Rican radio station plays the national Anthem every morning at 7:00 a.m.

Some **ornithologists** say that Costa Rica is the hummingbird capital of the world!

The largest uninhabited island in the world is Costa Rica's Isla del Coco. It is 360 miles (600 km) from the Pacific coast of Costa Rica.

In the small fishing village of Manzanillo, Costa Rica, there is a road called "Mista Cracker Jack Street."

The sun rises and sets in Costa Rica at the same time every day of the year. Can you guess why?

As of 2014, Claudia Poll and her sister Silvia are the only two Costa Ricans to win a medal in the Olympics. They both won medals in swimming events.

Life in Costa Rica:
"Pura Vida"

WHAT IS LIFE LIKE in Costa Rica? The answer can be found in two words: "Pura Vida": (pronounced: poo-ra vee-da). It means "pure life" or "good life." It's the national motto of Costa Rica. It also describes the Costa Rican way of life. It is a phrase you hear often in stores and on the street. When someone asks "How are you?" (Cómo estás) in Costa Rica, the answer is often "Pura Vida."

Tico Time

What time is it? If you're in Costa Rica, the answer is simple. "It's Tico Time!" Tico time? What's that? Well, you see, Costa Ricans have a habit of always arriving late – whether it's for a dinner or a business meeting or any kind of appointment. It's a habit that has become known as "Tico time" – arriving anywhere from 30 to 60 minutes late. So we have just one question: Do kids in Costa Rica arrive at school on tico time?

How to Speak Spanish in Costa Rica

Hello
(oh-lah)
Hola

My name is...
Mi nombre es ____.
(may nombre-es____)

How cool!
Qué chiva!

(kay-chee-ba)

Background photo:
Arenal Volcano

How are you?
Cómo estás?
(koh-moh est ahs)?

Yes
Sí
(see)

No
No
(no)

Good Bye
Adiós
(ah-dee-OHS)

Que Pega!
In American, we say, "He's a stick in the mud."
In Costa Rica, Ticos say "Que Pega!" (What a stick!)
Either way, it means the same thing: That person is pretty boring!

What's to Eat?
The Food in Costa Rica

DO YOU EVER HAVE A CRAVING for a hamburger and French fries? Or maybe a hot dog or a slice of pizza? Those are some popular foods in America, right?

Costa Ricans also crave their favorite food. It's called **gallo pinto** *(pronounced: gah-yo pin toe)*. It's a mixture of white rice and black beans cooked with a variety of fresh herbs and vegetables. Costa Ricans have gallo pinto at least once a day – often at breakfast with eggs and a tortilla. (Say: *tor **ti** ə.*)

For lunch or dinner, Costa Ricans often have a meal called *casado*. It consists of rice and beans (again), but this time served side by side rather than mixed together, along with beef or chicken.

Casado means "married man" in Spanish. So why is this traditional Costa Rican lunch called casado?

Christmas Tamales

SOMEONE ONCE SAID, "Every good Tico eats tamales for Christmas." And it's true. Tamales at Christmas time in Costa Rica are like turkeys at Thanksgiving in the U.S. It's a big part of the holiday.

The Christmas tamale is wrapped in large leaves with pork and/or chicken with rice and vegetables and special seasonings, tied with string, and boiled.

Did You Know? A **pulperia** is a small neighborhood grocery store, sort of like a deli.

School

ALL KIDS IN COSTA RICA have to go to school. They have six years of primary school and thee years of secondary school. The school year is divided into two terms. The first term runs from February to July; the other tem goes from August to November/ December. There is a two to three-week holiday at the end of the first term and a long holiday at the end of the second term. At the age of 15, students can enter college.

and Money

Money in Costa Rica is called the Colón (plural *colones*). The symbol of the Colón is a capital letter "C" crossed by two diagonal strokes. It looks like this: ₡. It's sort of like the U.S. dollar symbol: $.

Banknotes in Costa Rica – like the country itself – are fun and colorful. The front of each banknote features a famous Costa Rican. The back of each bill features one of Costa Rica's many animals.

Holidays in Costa Rica

IN THE UNITED STATES, we call it Columbus Day; in Costa Rica, it's called Día de las Culturas (*Day of Cultures*). But regardless of what it's called, the special day in October commemorates (or celebrates) the same thing – the arrival of Christopher Columbus in the New World. In Costa Rica, the holiday also honors the different cultures that make up the country.

There are other popular holidays and fiestas throughout the year in Costa Rica. Here are just two of the national holidays.

September 15: **Independence Day.** It's like our July 4th. On September 15, 1821, Costa Rica gained its independence from Spain. Today, on September 15, there are parades and festivities in every city and town and, like American's 4th of July celebration, there is a display of amazing fireworks.

July 25: **Annexation of Guanacaste Day.** On this day in 1824, the province of Guanacaste chose to become part of Costa Rica, rather than the neighboring country of Nicaragua. Every year, Costa Ricans celebrate this day with parades and festivities throughout the country.

FUTBOL (known as soccer in the United States) is by far the No. 1 favorite sport by all Costa Ricans – young and old alike. But there's another sport that some say is even more popular than fútbol. It's bullfighting – with a twist. . . **the bull is never hurt** – well, maybe a little annoyed. That's because at bullfights in Costa Rica, there is only one rule: *no one can hurt the bull.* But the bull...well, that's a different story.

Tico-style bullfighters get ready to take their chances with a mad bull at the Fiestas de Zapote in San Jose, Costa Rica.

The largest and most popular bullfights each year are held during the Fiestas de Zapote (or Zapote Festival) in a town outside San José. It's like the World Series and Super Bowl all rolled into one.

Hundreds of men (and some women) enter the bullring where the bull is. They annoy the bull by pulling its tail or spanking it. Then, they run like heck to avoid getting trampled (or worse) by the bull.

A fun time is had by all – so they say.

Costa Rican Wildlife

IF YOU LIKE BUTTERFLIES, you'll love Costa Rica. More than 10 percent of all known butterflies can be found in this tropical country.

But that's not the only wildlife you'll find here. Costa Rica is said to have the largest variety of wildlife of any other country in the world. Here is what you might see there:

894 bird species, more than all of the United States and Canada combined.

225 reptiles, including 20 **venomous** snakes.

175 different kinds of **amphibians**, 85% of which are frogs.

Eye lash viper

Scientists believe that the large, bright red "peppers" are one way the red-eyed tree frog scares away ***predators.***

2 species of sloths, *both of which spend nearly their entire lives hanging upside down in a tree. They even give birth upside down.*

Of course, there are monkeys. You can read about the four different kinds on the next page

The Rainforests of Costa Rica

WHAT'S THE DIFFERENCE BETWEEN a rainforest and a regular forest? The answer is probably obvious. Rain!

Some of Costa Rica's rainforests get as much as 80 to 260 inches of rain every year. Compare that to the state of Arizona. It gets only about 7 inches of rain each year.

The tropical rainforests of Costa Rica are known as the "jewels of the earth." They are home to two-thirds of all living animal and plant species.

A fun way to see a rainforest is on a zip-line. A zip-line consists of steel cables strung high across the canopy between two trees. Platforms are at either end to "take off" and land on. Hold your breath and away you go!

The Four Levels of the Rainforest And the Animals Who Live There

IN ANY RAINFOREST, there are four different levels.

The Forest Floor. Very little sunlight ever reaches the forest floor. But thousands of anteaters, lizards, rodents, and insects crawl around on the Forest Floor.

The Understory. This is a dark, cool area above the ground, but below the leaves. The red-eye tree frog and many different butterflies live in the Understory.

The Forest Canopy. This is the upper part of the trees. Monkeys, three-toed sloths, and many different birds live in the Canopy.

Emergents. These are very tall trees that rise high above the forest canopy. Scarlet Macaws live in the Emergent layer.

Monkey Around in Costa Rica

WANT TO HAVE more fun than a barrel of monkeys? Then Costa Rica is the place to go – to watch the monkeys, of course! There are four specific kinds (or species) of monkeys in Costa Rica.

The SHY **Central American squirrel monkey** is the smallest of the Costa Rican monkeys.

*The population of the shy **Central American squirrel monkey** is decreasing largely because of **deforestation**, hunting, and pet trade. Squirrel monkeys make 25 to 30 different and distinct noises when searching for food and when they feel threatened.*

Monkey Around in Costa Rica

The FRANTIC **capuchin monkey** (aka the white-faced monkey for obvious reasons).

The **capuchin monkey** loves fresh ripe fruit, so they smell it and squeeze it first before biting into it. They also like shellfish and crack the shells of shellfish with stones.

Monkey Around in Costa Rica,

The **NOISY** **mantled howler monkey,** which is famous for its howl. It can be heard nearly 1 mile (1.6 km) away.

*There are more **noisy mantled howler monkeys** in Costa Rica than any other monkey.*

Monkey Around in Costa Rica

The LARGE **spider monkey** is the largest monkey in Costa Rica.

The **spider monkey** can weigh as much as 20 pounds (9 kg) with arms that are much longer than its legs. Its tail is also longer than its body and head.

Did You Know?

Trees in Costa Rica's many rainforests can grow up to 100 feet (30 meters) tall.

National Hero: Juan Santamaría

The statue of Juan Santamaría with a torch in one hand and his rifle in the other stands as a symbol of national freedom in Costa Rica.

APRIL 11 IS AN IMPORTANT DAY in Costa Rica. It's a national holiday, like Martin Luther King Jr. day in the United States. It honors a national hero named Juan Santamaría.

In 1856 foreign invaders were trying to conquer Costa Rica. In one important battle, the Costa Rican army was losing. The enemy had the advantage. They were in a building near the center of town.

The general of the Costa Rican army needed someone to carry a torch to the building and set it on fire. The young Santamaría volunteered. Sadly, he was **mortally** wounded on his way. But he still managed to throw the torch and set fire to the building. As a result, the Costa Rican army was then able to drive the enemy out of town and win the battle.

Juan Santamaría was only 25 years old at the time.

Amphibian: A small animal that is born in water and then lives on land for part of its life.

Canopy: The overlapping branches and leaves of rainforest trees; the area of a rainforest where most plant and animal life is found in a rainforest (as opposed to the forest floor).

Deforestation: The cutting down of a large group of trees from an area of land.

Descendant: Someone who is related to a person or group of people who lived in the past.

Mortally: In a deadly or fatal manner.

Ornithologist: A person who studies birds.

Predator: An animal that eats the flesh of other animals.

Species: A particular group of things, such as a group of animals or plants, that are similar and can produce young animals or plants.

Symbolize: To represent or stand for something by means of a sign or object.

Venomous: Poisonous; able to inflict a poisonous bite or sting.

For Beginning Readers
The Elephant Picture Book

Curious Kids Press

The Elephant Picture Book

With original photography of the elephants at Boon Lott's Elephant Sanctuary in Thailand.

Ages 4-7

By Jack L. Roberts
With Photography
by Michael Owens

Available as E-book or Print Edition!

Other Books from Curious Kids Press

www.curiouskidspress.com

PlanetKids Series (ages 7-9)

PlanetKids: Ancient Egypt

PlanetKids: Australia

PlanetKids: Costa Rica

PlanetKids: France

PlanetKids: Kenya

PlanetKids: Thailand

A Kid's Guide to.. Series (ages 9-12)

A Kid's Guide to Ancient Egypt

A Kid's Guide to Australia

A Kid's Guide to China

A Kid's Guide to Costa Rica

A Kid's Guide to France

A Kid's Guide to Kenya

A Kid's Guide to Thailand

Other CKP eBooks for Kids

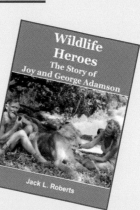

A Kid's Guide to
Costa Rica
For Parents and Teachers

About This Book

A Kid's Guide to . . . is an engaging, easy-to-read e-book series that provides an exciting adventure into fascinating countries and cultures around the world for young readers. Each book focuses on one country and includes colorful photographs, informational charts and graphs, and quirky and bizarre "Did You Know" facts, all designed to bring the country and its people to life. Designed primarily for recreational, high-interest reading, the informational text series is also a great resource for students to use to research geography topics or writing assignments.

About the Reading Level

A Kid's Guide to . . . is an informational text series designed for kids n grades 4 to 6, ages 9 to 12. For some young readers, the series will provide new reading challenges based on the vocabulary and sentence structure. For other readers, the series will reinforce reading skills already achieved. While for still other readers, the series text will match their current skill level, regardless of age or grade level.

About the Author

Jack L. Roberts began his career in educational publishing at Children's Television Workshop (now Sesame Workshop), where he was Senior Editor of The Sesame Street/Electric Company Reading Kits. Later, at Scholastic Inc., he was the founding editor of a high-interest/low-reading level magazine for middle school students. Roberts is the author of more than a dozen biographies and other non-fiction titles for young readers, published by Scholastic Inc., the Lerner Publishing Group, and Benchmark Education. More recently, he was the co-founder of WordTeasers, an educational series of card decks designed to help kids of all ages improve their vocabulary through "conversation, not memorization."